Giant Pandas

NOV 2013

by Marcia S. Freeman

Consulting Editor:
Gail Saunders-Smith, Ph.D.

Consultant:
Don Middleton, Member
International Association for
Bear Research and Management

Pebble Books

an imprint of Capstone Press
Mankato, Minnesota

Pebble Books are published by Capstone Press
1710 Roe Crest Drive, North Mankato, Minnesota 56003
www.capstonepub.com

 Books published by Capstone Press are manufactured with paper
containing at least 10 percent post-consumer waste.

Library of Congress Cataloging-in-Publication Data
Freeman, Marcia S. (Marcia Sheehan), 1937–
    Giant pandas / by Marcia S. Freeman.
    p. cm.—(Bears)
    Summary: Simple text and photographs describe the appearance, food, and
homes of the giant panda.
    ISBN-13: 978-0-7368-0098-3 (hardcover)
    ISBN-10: 0-7368-0098-0 (hardcover)
    ISBN-13: 978-0-7368-8099-2 (softcover pbk.)
    ISBN-10: 0-7368-8099-2 (softcover pbk.)
    1. Giant pandas—Juvenile literature. [1. Giant panda. 2. Pandas.] I. Title.
II. Series.
    QL737.C14.F74 1999
    599.789—dc21   98-19959

Note to Parents and Teachers

Books in this series may be used together in comparative activities to investigate differe
types of bears. The series supports the national science education standards for units on
the diversity and unity of animal life. This book describes and illustrates the appearance
and activities of the giant panda of China. The photographs support early readers in
understanding the text. The sentence structures offer subtle challenges. This book
introduces early readers to vocabulary used in this subject area. The vocabulary is defin
in the Words to Know section. Early readers may need assistance in reading some word
and in using the Table of Contents, Words to Know, Read More, Internet Sites, and
Index/Word List sections of the book.

Printed in the United States of America in North Mankato, Minnesota.
042013   007253R

Table of Contents

Giant pandas have black fur and white fur.

Giant pandas have black fur around their eyes.

Giant pandas have black fur on their ears.

Giant pandas live in bamboo forests in China.

Giant pandas climb trees.

Giant pandas eat bamboo leaves and bamboo stems.

Giant pandas spend most of the day eating.

Female giant pandas have cubs during summer or autumn.

Giant pandas are endangered. Few giant pandas live in the wild.

Words to Know

bamboo—a tall grass with a tough stem

cub—a young bear

endangered—in danger of dying out

female—a person or animal that can give birth or lay eggs

forest—a large area covered with trees and plants

fur—the hairy coat of an animal

leaf—the flat and usually green part of a plant that grows out from a stem

stem—the long part of a plant from which leaves and flowers grow

wild—an area that is in its natural state; giant pandas live in bamboo forests in China.

Read More

Duden, Jane. *The Giant Pandas of China.* Animals of the World. Mankato, Minn.: Hilltop Books, 1998.

Dudley, Karen. *Giant Pandas.* The Untamed World. Austin, Texas: Raintree Steck-Vaughn, 1997.

Feeney, Kathy. *Pandas for Kids.* Wildlife for Kids. Minocqua, Wis.: NorthWord Press, 1997.

Fowler, Allan. *Giant Pandas: Gifts from China.* Rookie Read-About Science. Chicago: Children's Press, 1995.

Internet Sites

Do you want to find out more about giant pandas? Let FactHound, our fact-finding hound dog, do the research for you.

Here's how:

1) Visit *http://www.facthound.com*

2) Type in the **Book ID** number: **0736800980**

3) Click on **FETCH IT**.

FactHound will fetch Internet sites picked by our editors just for you!

Index/Word List

Word Count: 72
Early-Intervention Level: 9

Editorial Credits
Michelle L. Norstad, editor; Clay Schotzko/Icon Productions, cover designer;
  Sheri Gosewisch, photo researcher

Photo Credits
Animals Animals/Mark Stouffer, 18
Dembinsky Photo Assoc. Inc., 14, 16, 20
Lynn M. Stone, 4, 6, 8, 10, 12
Root Resources/Kenneth W. Fink, cover; Alan G. Nelson, 1